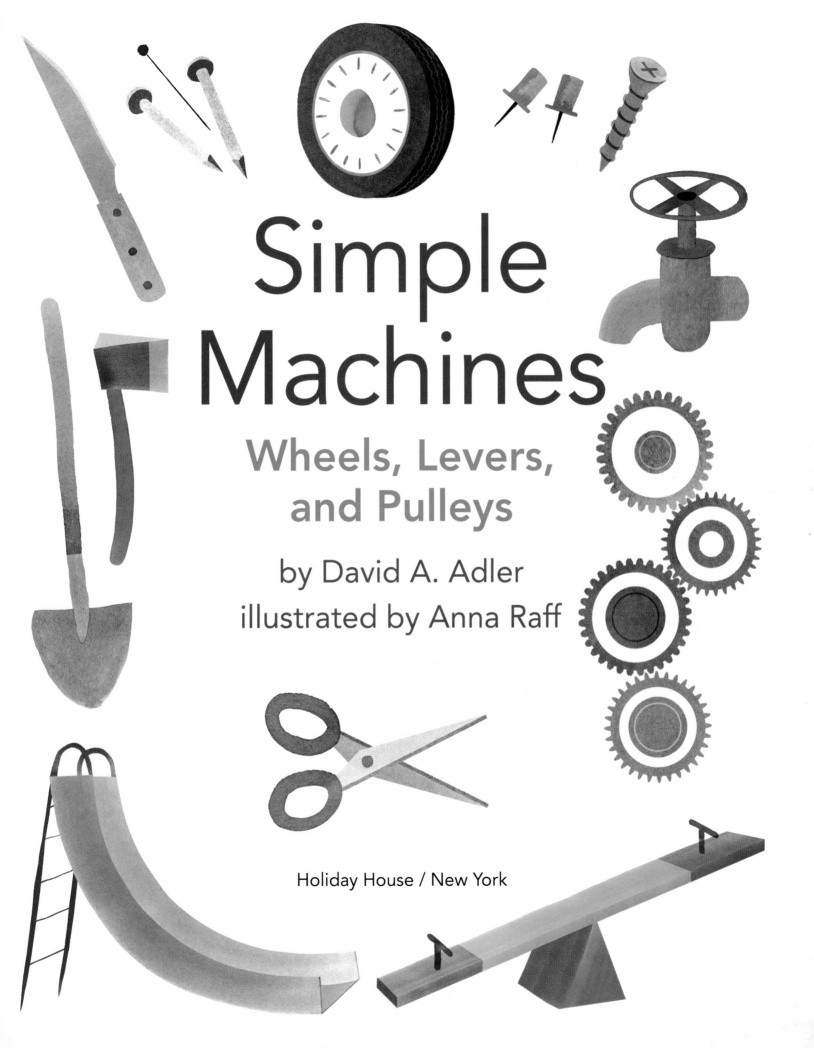

Simple Machines

Wheels, Levers, and Pulleys

by David A. Adler

illustrated by Anna Raff

Holiday House / New York

Machines make work easier.

Look in a mirror. Smile. You are looking at a whole set of simple machines, a whole set of wedges. A **wedge** is thin at one end and wide at the other. It's a simple machine that helps break things apart.

Your teeth are wedges. When you bite into an apple, the sharp, thin end of your teeth split the apple. Your teeth change the up-and-down direction of your bite into a sideways force that splits the apple into pieces small enough to swallow.

An ax is also a wedge. A lumberjack drives his ax into a log. He swings his ax down, and the log splits apart.

The force of the lumberjack's swing drives the wedge into the log. The wedge changes the downward direction of the force into a sideways force that breaks the log into smaller pieces.

A pair of scissors is a pair of wedges that work together. Thumbtacks, pins, nails, shovels, forks, knives, and chisels are also wedges. Many boats are wedges too. The front is narrow so it can push easily through the water.

Have you ever played on a slide? If you have, you played on a simple machine.

Stand at the top of a slide and look down. It's a hard drop straight down, but sliding down is not hard at all. It's fun.

A slide is an **inclined plane**, sometimes called a **ramp**.
It's a flat surface with one end higher than the other.
An inclined plane makes it easier to climb up and
down. It makes it easier to carry things up or down.

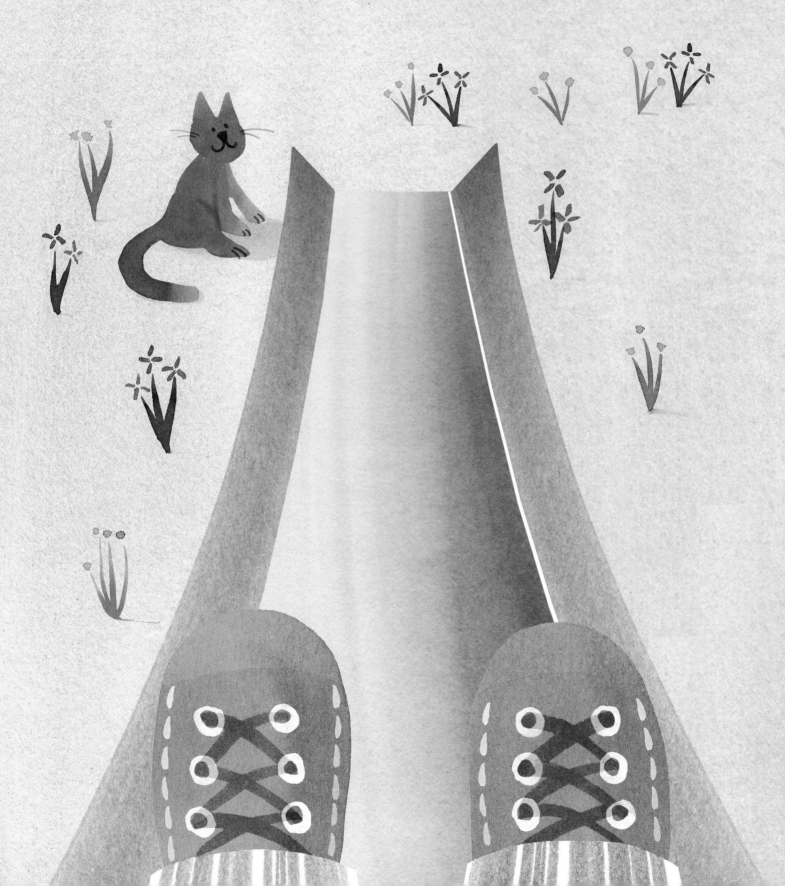

Imagine having to lift a box loaded with bowling balls.
Lifting the box would be difficult. Pushing it up a ramp
would be easier. The more gradual the slope of the
ramp, the easier the work. Of course, the more gradual
the slope, the farther you have to push the box.

THE CAT BOWL

An inclined plane gets the same work done with less force over a greater distance.

Roads often twist around mountains. The roads would be shorter if they went straight up. But a road that went straight up a mountain would be too steep to drive. Mountain roads are inclined planes.

The more gradual the slope of a mountain road, the easier the drive. But the more gradual the slope of a mountain road, the greater the distance you have to drive to reach the top.

Inclined planes are used to load trucks and to make it easier for people in wheelchairs to get around.

A screw is an inclined plane around a straight metal nail.

It would take a great force to push a nail into a piece of wood. Turning and pushing a screw into the wood is easier. When you push and turn a screw, you are moving it in along a circular inclined plane.

Have you ever played on a seesaw? If you have, you played on a **lever**, a simple machine.

⟵ load

A lever has two parts, a solid bar and a pivot. A pivot is sometimes called a fulcrum. On a seesaw, the long board with a seat at each end is the solid bar. The platform in the center doesn't move. It's the pivot.

The person on the other end of the seesaw may weigh as much as you do or more. But with a seesaw you can lift your friend easily. That's because a seesaw is a lever. It's a simple machine that makes lifting easier.

effort →

← pivot

A shovel can be a lever.

Find a shovel with a long handle. Take it to a sandbox or to a beach. First load the shovel with sand, hold both hands at the far end of the handle, and lift. It's difficult. The load feels really heavy.

pivot

Now leave one hand at the end of the handle and move one to the middle and lift. The load feels lighter.

pivot

Your hand at the end of the handle is providing the lifting force. Your hand in the middle is the pivot. You're using the shovel as a lever, and it's making it easier to lift the sand.

Have you ever tried to
move something heavy?

It's difficult to push or pull a heavy box along the ground. It's the **friction**—the rubbing of the bottom of the box against the ground—that makes moving the box so difficult.

It's a lot easier to move the box if it's in a wagon. It's the wheels and axles on the wagon that make your work easier.

A **wheel and axle** is just a large wheel attached to a small wheel. The small wheel is the axle. A wheel and axle is a simple machine. Wheels reduce friction.

Only the very bottoms of the wheels on a wagon touch the ground. That's a lot smaller area than the bottom of the entire box. With less rubbing on the ground, there's less friction.

 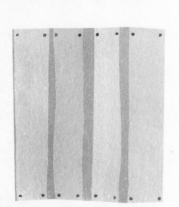

A wheel and axle also
multiplies the distance
something turns.

Have you ever been to an amusement park? Have you ever been on a Ferris wheel? A Ferris wheel is a good example of how wheels and axles multiply the distance something turns.

The axle in the middle of a Ferris wheel is attached to the motor. The motor supplies the power that turns the axle. The axle turns the Ferris wheel. The axle is just a small wheel. It doesn't make a big circle when it makes one complete turn. But the attached Ferris wheel does make a big circle. In one complete turn of a Ferris wheel, each seat on the wheel goes a long way.

On a Ferris wheel, the distance the axle turns is multiplied.

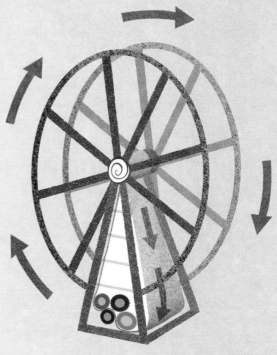

A wheel and axle can also be used, not to multiply the distance a wheel turns but to multiply the force used to turn the axle. You do that every day.

Every time you turn on a faucet you are turning a wheel and axle.

The faucet knob is the wheel. It's attached to a **shaft**, a thin rod that turns the water on and off. That thin shaft is the axle. Turning the shaft would be very difficult. The knob is larger and easier to turn because the knob multiplies the turning force. The larger the knob, the easier it is to turn the thin shaft.

Some wheels are attached to the axle. Some are not.

The front wheel of a tricycle is attached to the axle. The axle is attached to the peddles. When riders turn the peddles of their tricycles, they are turning the axles that turn the front wheels. It's the front wheels that pull the tricycles forward.

The back wheels of a tricycle are not attached to the axle. They spin around it.

Many machines need gears to make them work. A **gear** is a wheel with teeth. Gears can change the speed, power, and direction of a machine's work.

Combine a wheel and axle with some rope and you have a **pulley**, another simple machine.

A flagpole uses a pulley. The pulley is at the very top of the pole. You don't have to climb up the pole to raise the flag. You just pull down on the rope and the flag goes up. The pulley at the top of the pole changed the direction of your pulling force. For every foot of rope you pull down, the flag rises one foot.

A flagpole uses a fixed pulley. It's fixed—attached—to the top of the pole.

Many curtains and window blinds also use fixed pulleys.

What if you added a pulley, one that moved up and down with the flag. Now you are using two pulleys. You have to pull the rope farther to get it around both pulleys. You have to pull it more than one foot to raise it that much. But the pulling is easier.

The more pulleys you add, the less force you need.

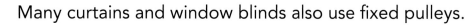

The next time you pass a construction site, look at the cranes, the large machines used to lift heavy objects. You'll see a pulley, probably several, between the top of the crane and whatever it's lifting. With the pulleys, the motor in the crane needs less lifting power.

For Zachary, Joshua,
and Benjamin
—D. A. A.

For Lee,
and the brilliant machine
between his ears
—A. R.

Text copyright © 2015 by David A. Adler
Illustrations copyright © 2015 by Anna Raff
All Rights Reserved
HOLIDAY HOUSE is registered in the U.S. Patent and Trademark Office.
Printed and Bound in October 2014 at Toppan Leefung, DongGuan City, China.
The artwork was created with sumi ink washes, assembled
and colored digitally with other media.
www.holidayhouse.com
First Edition
1 3 5 7 9 10 8 6 4 2

Library of Congress Cataloging-in-Publication Data
Adler, David A.
Simple machines : wheels, levers, and pulleys / by David A. Adler ; illustrated by Anna Raff. — First edition.
pages cm
Audience: Ages 4-8.
Audience: Grades K-3.
ISBN 978-0-8234-3309-4 (hardcover)
1. Simple machines—Juvenile literature.
I. Raff, Anna, illustrator. II. Title.
III. Title: Wheels, levers, and pulleys.
TJ147.A4154 2014
621.8—dc23
2014026802